How to Thrive in a Crisis:

A Practical Guide on How Businesses Can Succeed in Times of Adversity

Adam D. Korik

Copyright © 2020 by Adam D. Korik

All rights reserved. This book or any portion thereof
may not be reproduced or used in any manner whatsoever
without the express written permission of the publisher
except for the use of brief quotations in a book review.

adamdkorik@gmail.com

Contents

Introduction 1
I. SPS-System 5
   1. Strategic Management 7
   2. Business Process Modelling 14
   3. Organizational and Functional Structure (OFS) 20
II. Setting Up Control Systems 23
Conclusion 25

Introduction

The *crisis*... many are scared of this word, but now they fear what will happen next...

But why? Do these expectations emerge out of cognitive biases?

If you look at the issue from this point of view, you can see that not all companies are downsizing or bankrupt. There are many examples in the market where companies are announcing the expansion and recruitment of new employees, while increasing their volume and quality. Yes, you yourself can give many such examples, and not only in the fields of IT and e-commerce.

If other people can do it, why can't you?

Someone may argue that this is an exception to the rule. Yes, but this also means that these rules are not so concrete.

What are these companies? According to my observations, they are those who were able to ignore common concepts, find new opportunities, rebuild and move forward.

A good **example** would be a publishing company specializing in accounting and finance holding a significant market share before the 2008 crisis. The company went with the flow, facing several months of delays in numbers. However, when the crisis began, it became obvious that clients were not satisfied with this situation: they were not ready to pay for outdated information. The loss of clients began.

The fact is that before, all the work depended on the editors: they were completely responsible for everything (sound familiar?), from content to release. And, of course, the human factor could not help affecting the publication.

In the course of the work, the fundamental methods of approaching things were changed: the editors began to only deal with the analysis of regulatory legal acts, company problems, "cut" situations (situational approach) and distributing them between publications.

The referents (who did not exist before), having technical specifications, worked with the authors of the articles to determine the terms and quality of writing. It should be said that it became easier for authors to work with a specific request.

Based on this, new business processes were modelled and an appropriate organizational structure was built for them.

And, as a result, the client base began to grow, the line of publications expanded, staff expansion was announced, and, most importantly, the magazine issues began to not only come out on time, but also with relevant information.

I can provide such examples in different industries: advertising, logistics, trade, manufacturing, etc.

This example is not a miracle or a motivating story, but the fruit of purposeful work. This is what will be discussed in this book.

I. SPS-System

In the process of working with clients, we began to build all subsystems, integrate them with each other and create a single system.

We concluded that in a single organism, which a company is, all elements must be interconnected.

We observe a similar thing in the human body: even the left ear is somehow connected with the right heel! However, modern medicine considers a person as a set of organs and systems, hence the specialization of doctors: ENT, ophthalmologist, neuropathologist, surgeon, etc. I am not just a set of organs, but a single organism!

From this position, we began to consider companies a whole (even the words themselves are almost identical: organism and organization!), having built an interconnected system.

As a result, we created a model that was named SPS-system (strategy, processes, structure). The enlarged model looks like this:

Figure 1.
Integrated company management system (SPS-system).

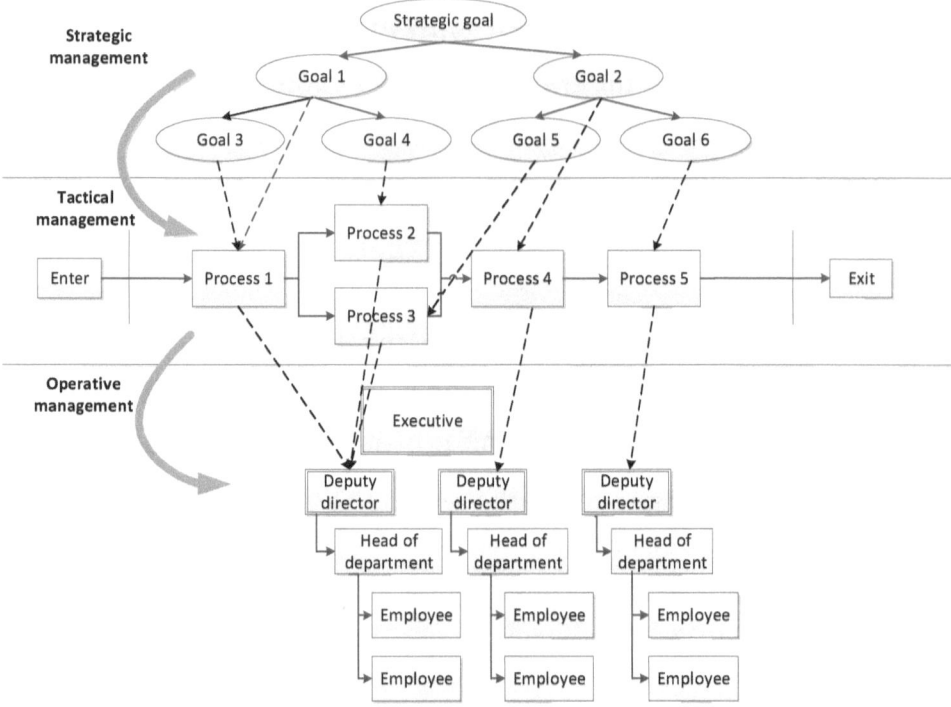

In a nutshell, the system looks like this:

- The organizational structure should be built in such a way that it facilitates an easy flow of business processes.
- Business processes should be built, in turn, in such a way as to help the organization achieve its goals.
- Based on these principles, all other systems and organizational links are built.

The step-by-step implementation scheme is as follows:

1. Strategic Management
2. Business Process Modelling
3. Organizational and Functional Structure (OFS)
4. Setting up Control Systems

The purpose of this book is to familiarize readers with the capabilities of the SPS-system integrated enterprise management system and the methods of its implementation. For those who find this system perfect for themselves, step-by-step detailed actions with drawings, diagrams and methodology will be presented in the future.

Now, let's consider each area of work in more detail.

1. Strategic Management

To develop this area of work, we applied the Balanced Scorecard approach (hereinafter: BSC) (R. Kaplan, D. Norton).

It should be noted that the BSC is an excellent tool for implementing the strategy, i.e. the strategy must have already been created. Considering the fact that in order to develop or change a strategy, you need:

- resources (financial, human), and
- time (for different organizations, this period can vary from 1 to 6 months or more)

Many companies have limited or no such resources at all, it is recommended to apply this stage in a simplified and accelerated form. Of course, this is not the best option; however, due to the problems faced by enterprises (crisis, pandemic), this is a forced measure. While the strategy is being developed, there will be nothing and nobody to implement. We will continue talking about this in the "Business Processes" chapter.

Let's assume you have a strategy. To implement it, it is necessary to conduct the following work:

- develop a goal tree
- create a BSC map
- develop key performance indicators (hereinafter: KPI)

Goal Tree

To create a complete picture of what the company should strive for in all key areas, it is necessary to:

- determine the correct set of levels that reflect the needs and specifics of the company
- create a sufficient and necessary set of goals
- divide targets by levels
- build causal relationships

According to the original source, the main planes are:
- finance
- customers and markets
- internal processes
- learning and growth

In the course of work, we have allowed ourselves to somewhat deviate from the original one. In many companies, we have found that learning and growth are necessary but not sufficient. Therefore, we changed this level to "potential", by which we mean not only these concepts, but also the items that are critical for organizations (transport, office equipment, computers with requirements, servers, software, utility systems, communication equipment, etc.).

Example: When conducting business diagnostics of a logistics company, we saw a problem in the quality of customer service. In the course of the work, we found out that operators need faxes for operational work. However, faxes were located in a remote spot. As a result, operators had to spend time transmitting information, and in turn were receiving documents with a delay. By installing faxes on operators' desks, the quality and terms of service have improved significantly. It would seem such an obvious and small problem, but, not seeing its consequences, management did not solve it. The decision came after analysing the Infrastructure level, where the need to provide internal processes with the necessary equipment was identified.

Figure: 2.
An example of a goal tree

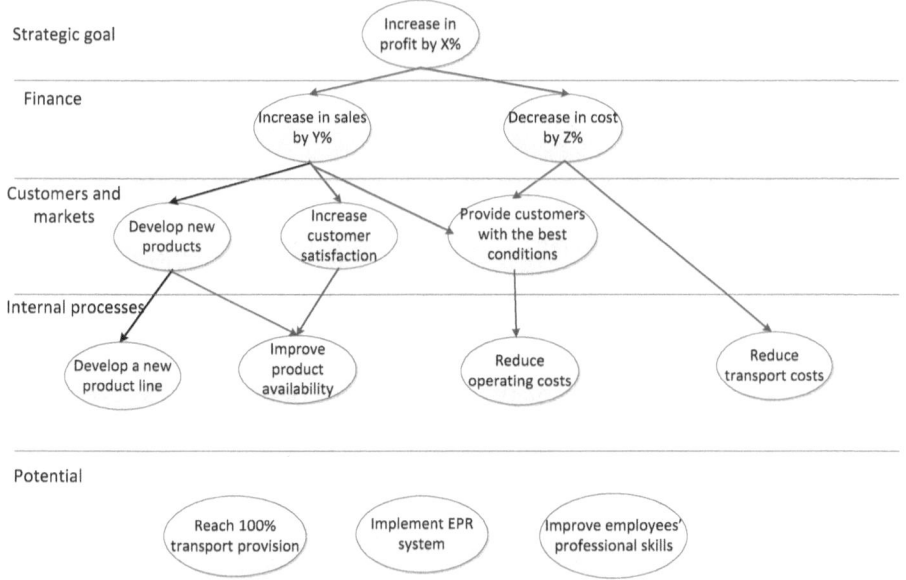

1. Basically, the set of levels and their order are defined as above. However, there are also specific moments. For example, for a company that generates harmful emissions, it may be necessary to include the "Ecology" level; for government and non-profit organizations, it is possible to change the order of levels: customers and markets become first and finance goes to the third position.

2. Having created a set and sequence of levels, it is necessary to isolate the goals from the strategy and distribute them along the levels.

Attention! In the goal tree, all goals are equally important. If the goal is on the third level, "Internal Processes", this does not mean that it is less important than the goal in the first level. Both of them need to be given sufficient attention.

3. Build a cause-effect relationship between them. It is obvious that almost all goals are somehow related to each other. Here it is necessary to identify the most important and critical relationships.

The logic for constructing cause-effect relationships between levels and goals is as follows:

- What financial goals should we achieve in order to achieve the strategic goals?
- How can we build relationships with customers and markets so that they trust us with their money, and we, accordingly, achieve financial goals?
- How do we need to build internal processes in order to meet customer needs at the required level?
- What kind of support do we need in order for internal processes to work at the proper level?

Create a BSC Map

The BSC map looks like this:

Figure: 3.
BSC Map

№	Goals	Objectives	Activities	Indicators	Unit of measure	Ratio	Permissible deviation	Collection frequency	In charge
1	Increase in sales by Y%								
2	Decrease in cost by Z%								
3	...								

1. When developing a BSC map, all goals are recorded in the right column.
2. For each goal, tasks are determined that must be completed in order to achieve the goal.
3. Tasks are broken down into activities, the implementation of which will lead to the solution of the problem.
4. Set up a necessary and sufficient set of indicators that fully characterize the implementation (or non-implementation) of activities.

Attention! The indicators should be fairly simple and inexpensive to obtain. There have been cases when, in order to obtain an indicator, it was necessary to carry out work where cost and time outweighed its value. For example, the frequency and necessity of conducting a customer satisfaction survey should be assessed in terms of feasibility and cost.

5. Determine the frequency of collection and permissible deviations for each level of management responsible for the measurement and achievement of indicators, in the future—to make a connection to business processes and the corresponding organizational link.
6. For each indicator, a card is created, where they are numbered and where all its parameters are reflected.

Note: Companies are often confused about digitizing goals. For example, there was a goal like this:

Achieve higher customer satisfaction

This goal is difficult to assess in numbers, since all judgments will be subjective.

According to our methodology, we have broken this goal into tasks, and tasks into activities. The latter are already easy to digitize (simplified version):

Goals	Tasks	Activities	Indicators
Achieve higher customer satisfaction	Ensure information availability and attractiveness of the company	Increase the number and duration of sessions on the website	Number of site visits
			Average time on the site
	Improve the quality of services provided	Reduce the number of complaints	Number of complaints
		Increase the number of repeated requests	Number of repeated requests
		Reduce service delivery time	Average service delivery time

2. Business Process Modelling

As noted above, developing a strategy can be a labor-consuming and time-consuming process. In times of crisis, not all companies have the opportunity and time to create a complete strategy. Additionally, the strategies that worked before the start of the crisis often fail to meet the requirements of the current crisis.

In these cases, we resort to the development of the so-called simplified version, i.e. strategic directions—which can be formed in 2-7 days—on the basis of which a strategic map will be created. More on this will be described in the following books.

Based on our experience, there is no need to spend time and money to a model business process "as it is." A completely justified approach is modelling a business process "as it should."

In our practice, we limited ourselves to 3 levels of business processes for many reasons:

- This is a sufficient amount for a breakdown with the required detail.
- At the 3rd level, we can reach the level of functions—an indivisible part, the "building blocks" of an organization.

First, based on the understanding of strategic goals, the 1st level (corporate) is built, which describes:

- main processes (where added value is created)
- workflows and their sequence
- inputs (raw materials, information) that must be provided to create a quality product
- outputs—results of activities
- management processes
- supporting processes (finance, accounting, IT support, technical support, personnel management, etc.)

At the second level, all processes of the first level are broken down.

Attention! The optimal number of processes is 8-10 max, because a large number would be difficult to manage. Excessive detail at these levels should be avoided.

Important! After modelling the processes of the 2nd level, it is useful to defend each process in the 1st level by their leaders in front of the participants of other processes (both main and auxiliary). This will give a comprehensive and objective assessment, discussion of the correctness of inputs and outputs and the logic of their construction, which will avoid questions and difficulties in modelling processes of levels 2 and 3.

In principle, anyone can model business processes, even an external consultant. But we concluded:

- if I, a consultant, simulate the process myself, it will be 100% wrong
- if I simulate it together with a specialist, it will be half worked out

We came to this when we introduced the practice of defending all 1st level processes in front of all others. Moreover, not only subcontractors (internal suppliers and customers) participated, but also management and procurement processes. During the defence, unexpected questions arose from lawyers, financiers, IT specialists, etc. Having worked through them, we realized how important it is.

After understanding all the requirements for the process, the owner of the 1st level process can form the correct 2nd level processes.

For modelling the processes of the 1st and 2nd levels, we use the IDEF0 notation, and for the 3rd level, ARIS, slightly changing and adapting them to our methodology.

After the completion of work on process modelling, approvals are carried out with external contractors—suppliers and customers. Thus, we build our processes in such a way as to satisfy customer requests and set the correct requirements for suppliers.

The scheme for modelling business processes of levels 1 and 2 will look like this:

Figure 4.
The basic outline of Level 1 and Level 2 processes.

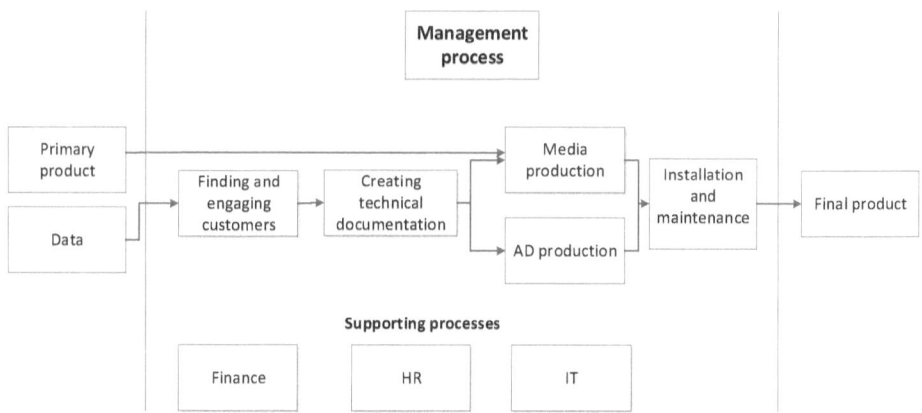

The arrows indicate the value-added streams. Due to the fact that the management and support processes interact with all processes without exception, in this case, they are simply denoted by rectangles. Their interaction is indicated at levels 2 and 3.

The scheme for modelling business processes of the 3rd level will look like this:

Figure 5.
An example of a 3-level process scheme.

Analysis of deliveries made with comments:

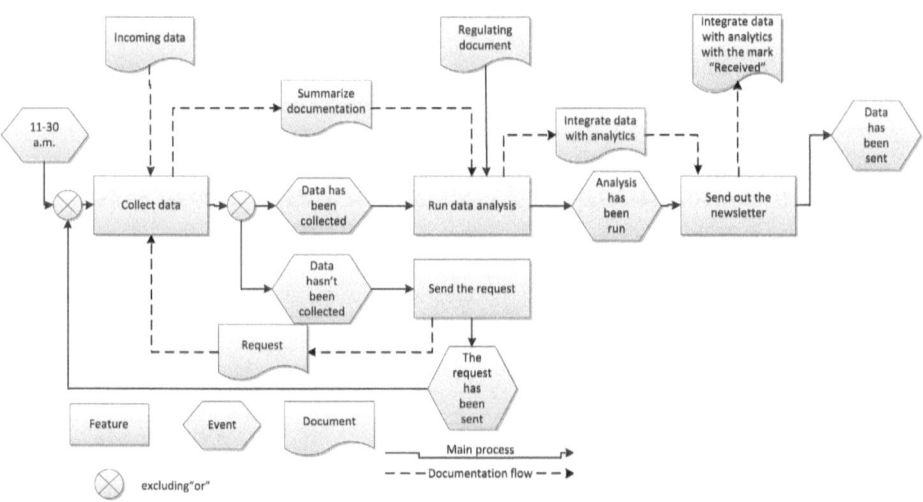

When modelling Level 3 processes, the following points should be considered:

1. Each level 3 process begins and ends with an event.

2. Functions alternate with events.

3. Workflows are written with a solid line, document flows with a dotted line.

4. Logical operators (logical "and", logical "or", exclusive "or") are placed before the event.

The difference between logical operators: logical "or" allows the execution of a function when at least one event occurs; logical "and" when all events occur; excluding "or" when only one event occurs.

5. Regulatory documents are attached to the functions so that an employee, even a new one, clearly understands what, how and why it should be done.

6. Indicate only important conditions for deviation from the normal course of the process.

7. In case of a deviation from the process, it is necessary to register the conditions for exiting the cycle (number of periods, time, etc.).

3. Organizational and Functional Structure (OFS)

As you have already seen, at the 3rd level of business processes, we split them into functions. They can be called atomic indivisible elementary particles. Actually, that's why we call the structure organizational-functional: the set of all functions of the 3rd level, interconnected in a certain way and logically combined into subdivisions, make up the organizational structure of the organization.

Depending on the processes and goals, different types of OFS can be built:

- linear
- linear-functional
- divisional
- matrix
- combined

The above are the most common types of OFS. Of course, they can be anything else; the main thing is that the requirement is being fulfilled: to help (and not interfere) with the flow of the business processes.

An important point: after modelling business processes, management does not need to come up with functional responsibilities and job descriptions; they are all already reflected in the processes of the 3rd level.

The set of functions performed by an employee will be his job description. This is used very well by managers and HR specialists: each employee can recruit the number of functions that meet his, and the employer's, goals.

For example, an employee who has small children, elderly parents, etc., does not have the opportunity to be loaded full time. He, having coordinated this with the manager, takes a set of functions that suit him, while, of course, reducing wages.

Another employee, on the contrary, wants to earn more (loans, mortgages, children, etc.). Then he gains such a number of functions that, as a result, his wages satisfy his needs.

Such working conditions were considered prior to the introduction of quarantine. Now, in a crisis and pandemic, we can consider the possibility of remote work, attracting freelancers, etc. It will be easier to implement, as well as control, because all processes are spelled out, the conditions of inputs and outputs are agreed, the quality parameters of the performance of functions are known to all parties (internal and external suppliers and customers, management, supporting processes).

Thus, the functions, when written, digitized in terms of time and money, serve as puzzles from which to build a picture—a thriving company.

II. Setting Up Control Systems

At this stage, it is necessary to link all 3 management planes (strategic, process and OFS). To do this, you must:

- Identify which processes are responsible for achieving the goals from the BSC map
- Link the KPIs developed in the BSC map with the processes of all three levels
- Align process indicators with organizational units and employees
- Fix all relationships and connections

After the development of the considered systems, their implementation is necessary. In the case of a discussion of all processes within the team and with subcontractors (suppliers and customers), as described above, this usually does not cause any difficulties.

Attention: Do not rush to automate these systems. Of course, this will speed up all the work, and make it more convenient. However, do not implement automation:

- Until all employees and departments are accustomed to the new processes (the changes can be quite big)
- Until all the unforeseen circumstances that have arisen are corrected (and they will certainly arise!)

After some time (you yourself will feel the difference)—usually after 6-12 months—both management and employees will notice that the processes can be performed better and the time spent can be reduced.

This will be the signal to start automation. Moreover, during this period, each employee will be ready to give an exhaustive technical specification for automation in his area.

Conclusion

Having built a company according to the principle described above, you will be able to flexibly respond to the challenges and requirements of the market, taking advantage of the strengths of each component of the system. As practice shows, after the transition to a new principle of work, employees themselves, at their level, begin to make the necessary changes in a timely manner, and management begins to correct deviations in advance. At the same time, the CEO of the company practically moves away from operational intervention in the processes and begins to concentrate on strategic issues.

The development period of the above systems—with a competent approach—can be 1-3 months for small and medium-sized businesses and 3-8 months for large businesses. Of course, these dates are very approximate. Much depends on the specifics of the industry, region, and other factors.

If you have any questions, I will be happy to answer by mail adamdkorik@gmail.com.

www.ingramcontent.com/pod-product-compliance
Lightning Source LLC
Chambersburg PA
CBHW031517210526
45464CB00007B/2960